Unruly

Poems
by
Ellen Summerfield

ISBN-13: 978-1979310987

ISBN-10: 197931098X

Cover art: *Irises* (1889) by Vincent van Gogh
Digital image courtesy of the Getty's Open Content Program.

Cover design: Nectar Graphics, McMinnville, OR
www.nectargraphics.com

Normality is a paved road: It's comfortable to walk,
but no flowers grow on it.
~van Gogh

For Phil

Hope is a very unruly emotion.
~Gloria Steinem

CONTENTS

Elsewhere and back

Play on, words

Some day

In the shade

Learn the rules like a pro, so you can break them like an artist.

~Pablo Picasso

Multiverse

I believe we exist in a multiverse of universes.
~Michio Kaku

Raisin d'être

Unable to decide between whole wheat and raisin,
I turn to the headlines and read: *Suddenly,*
Universe Gains 40 Billion More Galaxies.

Just as suddenly, I feel dizzy.
My mind swirls as I imagine spiral
after spiral spinning in emptiness,
bejeweling infinity.

I put on coffee and wait by the window,
thinking that if it were dark,
I'd go outside, look up,
and seek out my old friends,
the ones nearby,
like the dipper still pouring out
its fresh organic milk,
and the two whose names I loved to pronounce—
Cassiopeia and Betelgeuse.

It would feel good to see them again,
the eternal nocturnal neighbors
who've been up there since my childhood,
since those evenings when dad,
tired from work,
yet not wanting to disappoint,
would join me on the stoop
and hold the flashlight
over my *Big Book of Constellations*,
opened wide on my knees,
then point with me to the heavens
to greet the zoo animals, find Orion's belt,
and tell me that, yes, girls can be astronomers too.

Focusing my blurry morning eyes on the newspaper,
I find out that last week Hubble sent its telescopic eye
into the cosmos farther, deeper
than anyone has ever gone before,
taking pictures of galaxies so distant,
experts say, that they *stretch back*
toward the beginning of time.

My coffee ready,
I slouch in my chair
and ponder the vast affair,
having decided
on raisin.

Companions

Mythic Helena

I am Ellen
the daughter of Helene
who is the daughter of Sarah
who was the daughter of Helena.

Imperious Helena,
born to the wrong family
—Yiddish-speaking peasants with seven other children—
at the wrong time
for a woman of her temperament.

Her first marriage was for love.
We know little more, only that
he was a poet, they lived in a cold attic,
he died of tuberculosis.

Back at home, bereaved, aloof,
refusing to harvest potatoes,
Helena soon married Old Man Kaplan.
In the wedding photograph he looks like Tolstoy,
his beard resembling used tinsel,
his eyes clouded by time.

Sitting beside him, erect, the new bride,
her hair styled in an aristocratic bun on top of her head,
her frilled satin blouse fastened at the neck
by an enormous diamond brooch.
Boris Kaplan had money, but, judging from the photo,
he was too old for Helena,

who convinced him she needed a vacation
in America and took their infant Sarah,
dressed like a czarina, along with all her jewels,
on a first-class journey from Vilna to Baltimore.

Once there, she taught Hebrew school
and caught the attention of a wealthy man
from the synagogue. We know him as
Old Man Wiener, the year was 1908,
she was not yet thirty.

When she found herself pregnant,
she tried to abort the child, began to bleed,
and was rushed to Johns Hopkins,
where she died in the basement of the hospital
under the name of Ida Levine,
leaving Sarah homeless,
since her Old Man Wiener
didn't want her.

No one knows what happened
to Helena's jewels.

Sarah

Until I was grown I never had anything new,
my clothes were all hand-me-downs,
my Nana Sarah told me, *and I was such a big girl,*
nothing ever fit, dresses too tight, sleeves too short,
I should show you the photos I have,
I'm never smiling, looked like a beggar,
something out of Dickens, but I couldn't complain,
I was an orphan, you see,
Aunt Eva and Uncle Abe took me in,
they had two children of their own,
were poor as church mice,
but very kind.

Just as soon as she could, Sarah went to work,
first in an umbrella factory,
then as a salesgirl at Schleisner's,
starting at the bottom,
eventually becoming manager of women's coats,
so all the years I knew her
she was smartly dressed
in the latest fashions, with gloves and hats,
self-assured, on a first-name basis
with many of Baltimore's most influential women,
who made appointments with her
when the new shipments
of cashmere and mink coats arrived
and depended on her for advice.

Sarah had her own mink,
her own gold and diamond jewelry,
putting $5 a week on layaway
one item at a time until each new purchase
was hers to take home, care for, wear to work.

So when I was born, the first granddaughter,
she made sure I had bonnets and frilly dresses,
and I remember when she bought me
my mermaid nightgown,
the black patent leather Mary Janes I wanted so badly,
the heart locket engraved with my initials.

Before I moved away for college,
she took me shopping for an entire outfit—
a Villager kilt and sweater set, blue-green
to match my eyes, knee socks, penny loafers.
This is for your first day of class.

If I had a granddaughter,
I could hand down to her the fine gold bracelet
that Sarah, her great-great-grandmother, left me,
but, then again, would a young girl wear it
like I do, every day, or just put in in a drawer,
it's old-fashioned, filigree,
she might prefer the latest Apple Watch,
and, besides, it might cover one of her tattoos.

In the same shell #1

It's pretty much the same every week,
these glimpses into the lives of people
who have found each other, who almost always look like
they've made the right choices.

Daniella and Jordan III from exclusive private schools
becoming acquainted through their common interest
in lacrosse, or Nandini, a pediatrician, perfectly paired
with Niraj, trader of securities, to be wed
first in a traditional Hindu ceremony in Bombay,
then under a gazebo at the New Haven Lake Club.

And the more unusual one today: Peanut,
specialist in dental implants,
looking happy to be in the same shell with her Jason,
a champion chess player and senior manager at Microsoft.

I'm not sure why I read these announcements,
poring over them each Sunday in my *New York Times*,
perhaps because of their fairy-tale quality,
because these lives seem so perfect,
unlike mine, or those of anyone I know.

I wonder what would happen if you cracked them open,
looked inside. Is anything spoiled or rotten?
Would there be heartache and loneliness?
Has anyone been cheated, mistreated?

Or have they all been spared and graced,
their childhoods spent nestled with well-behaved siblings
in a secure home on a tree-lined street,
their married lives to be untouched by
birth defects, embezzlement, pyorrhea,
computer viruses, or Dutch Elm disease.

In the same shell #2

They, too, have found each other,
Heather and Derek,
gracing the pages of the *Asbury Park Press*
in their champagne moment,
before honeymooning in Vegas,
then returning to repair refrigerators
for Lowe's, to specialize in twists and braids
at *Perfect Look Salon*.

On the same page today, Sandy and Pete,
both from Manasquan,
who met at a high school dance,
he'll join his dad in construction,
she works part-time at *Tiny Tots* day care.

Their lives will not really mix with those
in the other shells, the ones written up in the *Times*,
unless Pete is called one day to fix the ice machine
in Nandini's freezer, or Sandy applies to be a nanny
and dog walker for Peanut and Jason,

or Daniella, driving home on an unfamiliar road
one night after a charity event, swerves to miss a deer,
and Derek, the first on the scene,
pulls her from her overturned car,
administering the CPR he learned as a summer lifeguard.

He doesn't want credit for saving her,
anyone would have done the same, he says,
he and Daniella won't stay in touch,
having little in common, but she's grateful,
aware that in the same situation her Jordan
would not have know what to do.

Touching tears

At Manhattan Judaica I once bought a *mezuzah*,
modern, the polished gray case
crescent-shaped, a metal biscotti,
with two identical doves perched on it,
one looking in, the other looking out,
and with its scrolled parchment—
verses from the Torah—tucked inside.

On returning to my small Oregon town,
I affixed it to my front doorpost,
but to be honest, I don't follow custom
by placing my hand on it, then kissing my fingers,
each time I enter the house,
and now that I think of it, I'm not even sure
what the Hebrew scripture says.

Nonetheless I love the idea of placing something
small and beautiful on my doorframe
to mark the passage between inside and out,
reminding me of the sacredness of home,
encouraging me to create peace when I step across.

Never having seen mezuzahs widely available,
I was surprised to find so many in Israel,
sold on every city block like newspapers,
some mass produced, unremarkable,
others stunning works of art,
with silver filigree, or gemstones, depicting
the twelve tribes, Biblical scenes, or the Holy Land,
worthy of museums, like the memorable piece
the dazzling silversmith Sari showed me in her studio,
uncannily similar to mine at home,
but, instead of birds, three indentations
engraved into the sterling surface,
the middle one larger than the other two.

I want to put my fingers inside them—
Sari says, yes, that's what she intended,
the three marks are the *touch
of the ages*, as if thousands of hands
throughout Jewish history have felt them,
reached for them for safety and blessing,
the pressure over time carving imprints,
as do feet on worn stone steps,

and I respond that they look like
tears,
so heavy that
they penetrate the metal.

I touch the tears as if to
wipe them away, but they
remain.

Wrapped in white

Before you leave, the silversmith Sari told me,
you must go to Motke's studio. He's an old man now,
a Holocaust survivor, a truly great artist.
Please do go see him.

Motke Blum, 85, an international figure,
was cordial but clearly agitated.
As Sari had just explained,
the *Hutzot Hayotzer* (Artists' Colony)—
an enchanting cobblestone lane near the Old City
where the public can meet master artisans
at work in their studios—
might not survive into the new year.

Earlier that month Motke had received an eviction
letter from Jerusalem's city hall, informing him
that his contract of forty years would not be renewed.
Along with all his neighbors in the colony,
he would have three weeks to empty his studio of his life's work

for expansion of the nearby Mamilla Mall,
a wildly successful upscale pedestrian shopping area
housing Lamborghini, Rolex, and the first Gap outlet
in Israel—a destination striving for the recognition
of Beverly Hills' Rodeo Drive.

I stayed only long enough to learn that
Motke had finally left behind
his palette of pain,
storing the paintings of previous years in a back room,
trading the dismal hues of the camps
for white,
all the shades of white,
luminous paintings done in this one color,
whites covering the canvases in strokes of light,

white possessing, in his words, a *royal simplicity*,
white holding within itself the entire spectrum—
white allowing him to *remove the layers of darkness*
in his search for renewal.

Having spent a lifetime
learning to wrap misery in white,
Motke will no doubt
gather his belongings and his
wits
and move on,
summoning a different
type of strength to face
this special brand of ruthlessness,
to contend with being
displaced by handbags,
driven out by convertibles,
exiled by strands of pearls.

**Feeling blue while reading *Architectural Digest*
in the dentist's office**

I pick up the top magazine on the pile,
the cover catching my eye with its caption,
The Good Life: Dazzling Homes around the World,
and its photo of an *earthly paradise*
set atop a dramatic cliff
overlooking the azure Aegean Sea.

Turning to the feature story inside,
I'm invited to
*breathe a sense of relaxation
in this most exclusive location.*

My dentist nowhere in sight,
I let Natalie M. guide me
through her fifteen-bedroom Burgundy chateau,
filled with 18th-century glories
and restored for $28.2 million
with glamorous entertaining in mind.

I thumb further and tour a fashion magnate's
grand four-story palazzo in Milan,
advised that when one owns this home
and several others around the world,
plus a stunning 213-foot yacht,
finding time to spend at each residence can be a challenge.

My tooth beginning to pound,
I set the magazine aside,
feeling dejected, not only about my cavity,
but there's something else—
what's wrong, what's making me sad,
then suddenly I realize,
I've got the *Architectural Digest* blues.

Feelin' blue while readin' some slick mag

Back molar's hurtin hurtin
Gonna die for certain certain
In a real bad bind
Bout to lose my mind
Got the low down pound pound toothache blues.

My doc is runnin late again
Don't care nothin bout my pain
My old guitar would help me now
I'd strum some bars, get through somehow

Dang tooth's achin achin
Whole body's shakin shakin
It's them low down pound pound toothache blues.

Gotta get a recess
From this doggone abscess
Pickin' up a magazine
One that I ain't never seen
Who the heck is Natalie
Lives like a queen in Burgundy
Whole dang thing depresses me.

Toothache pain's still hangin on
Man I want it gone gone gone
Now toppa that I gotta lose
These *Architectural Digest* blues.

German Lesson #1

The three past tenses—
simple past, present perfect, and past perfect—
are frightening,
telling of misdeeds that
were, have been, and had been carried out.

To form comparatives and superlatives of adjectives
 you add -er and -est, so one might say that
the twentieth century was *schrecklich* (terrible),
even *schrecklicher* than the previous one,
one of the *schrecklichsten* in world history.

The nouns are often composites—
long unpronounceable words like
Vergangenheitsbewältigung,
coming to terms with the past,

and then there are those pesky separable prefixes
that leave their verbs and walk off to the end
of the sentence, like *mitlaufen,* meaning
to go along with or join in (literally to run with)—
wenn sie Angst haben, laufen viele Menschen einfach mit
(when they're afraid, many people go along bad things with*)*,

just like the verbs that take a hike themselves
to the end of the phrase or clause—
machen wir jetzt Schluss für heute, weil ich etwas deprimiert bin,
let's stop for today, because I somewhat depressed am.

German Lesson #2

The present tense requires too many decisions.
Mistakes lurk everywhere, not at all like English,
where a verb hardly conjugates,
so I fail, you fail, she fails, we fail, they fail,
but in German the endings for *sheitern* change
with each pronoun, *ich scheitere, du scheiterst, er scheitert,
wir scheitern, ihr sheitert, sie scheitern,*

and if the verb is irregular, even the stem changes,
I collapse, *ich breche zusammen,*
you collapse, *du brichst zusammen,*
the entire EU is collapsing,
die Europäische Union bricht zusammen,
Germany being unable to
absorb the flow of refugees,
support the Euro,
lead the way through the European crisis.

That's enough for today, though,
ich habe Kopfweh, I have a headache,
we can't take on too much at once,
tomorrow we'll look into the future.

Agnosticism, a statement on my increasing

Not that I'd
shout
tout
or flout it
to the devout

but for me
it's all about
Doubt.

If you once let Doubt
sprout
it will
    break out
        branch out
                fill out
                  spread out.

Doubt loves to sprout.

Jocularity, a short sociological treatise on

Bringing levity to gravity
comedy to tragedy
may be seen as
impropriety.

What, you may ask,
could ever prompt frivolity
in the midst of calamity?

And yet
humanity needs
levity
to reduce anxiety

to preserve
sanity.

Appointment

For Tricia Crawford (1941-2013)

You wanted to keep your appointment
that Monday afternoon at 3 p.m.,

so Bob helped you dress
and drove you to the salon,

where you leaned your neck back
over the marble bowl, closed your eyes,

and felt the warm water on your scalp,
Mya's hands shampooing, caressing,

your head a frothy apple-scented lather.
She lingered this time over the massage,

then water once more and soy conditioner for silkiness,
for revitalization. A final rinse, the newborn feeling

of clean hair. She turbaned you in a plush green towel
and walked with you over to the swivel chair,

where you faced yourself in the mirror
and watched the silver fall to the floor

as she trimmed, shaped, fashioned. Now only
the drying remained, the airy fanning and fluffing,

and the brushing, like when we were little girls
and our mothers got out the tangles.

You left the salon unhurriedly, your head upright,
not scheduling your next appointment.

Square

From your bed
you can see out the window.

All of the outdoors is
reduced to a square.

Your garden comes in to you.
You trace the hourly progress

of the magnolia planted next to the house.
Now it cares for you, stands by you,

firm in its place, offering its blossoms.
The daytime skies are there for you too—

not the insistent cloudless blues of your childhood
but our northern grays, pale and soothing—

and at night the heavens
guiding your sleep, your way,

letting you know the darkness is not to be feared,
its size no more than a square.

Past tense

Eyeglass day

Once a year, Saturday 6 a.m.,
we'd pile into the station wagon
for our day out. Four of us in the back,
no seat belts, already bouncing, whining,
sniffling, punching. I'd plead carsickness
to get the window, to escape
the clammy feel of little brothers' skin
and the tadpole smell of boys.

Fear at the Holland Tunnel—
down into the darkness,
then Manhattan, we're here,
New York City, streets whizzing by
fast bicycles, rows and rows
of stores, delicatessens
yellow taxis racing with us
push down the door locks
still driving, making another turn
how does dad know
where to go? Red lights, relief
when I spy the big neon "P" atop
the sign announcing:
Bargain glasses $10
Made on the premises
Ready the same day.

Look for a parking space,
who wants to put coins in the meter?
A scramble up the steep,
poorly lit stairway to Pildes
on the second floor, to the chart
with the "E" for my name.

A tray of children's frames, black, plastic, oval,
pick any one. There's another tray
under the counter, pink frames
with sparkles, those cost too much,
then rushing over to push our noses
against the windows of the lab where
goggled men huddle over grinding machines,
they know how to make glasses.
Come back in an hour and they'll be ready.

We race ahead of mom and dad to the automat,
push our way inside, study the rows
of little glass doors, each one a choice,
decide on whatever we want,
drop nickels into the slots,
pull out a mac and cheese, a burger,
or a ham sandwich. We drink large Cokes with ice,
we're one big myopic family.

Back at Pildes, I tell myself
it doesn't matter that much.
Too old for tears, I wait my turn to get fitted
on the nose, behind the ears.
Can you see better now?

Dad takes out his weary wallet,
lays six crisp ten-dollar bills from the bank
on the counter one by one,
we're done, time to go before the meter runs out.

I walk to the stairs slowly,
looking down, careful
not to catch a view of myself
as I pass the mirrors.

Miss M.

Miss Helen McDonnell,
high school advanced English,
didn't spare us,
choosing world classics
one after the other by weight,
like the *Odyssey*,
and assigning Herculean amounts of homework,
but here the Schned twins had a big advantage,
since, as we all knew,
Ed Schned did one half and Ted Schned the other,
but I didn't really care,
having a major crush on them both.

When Miss M. turned her back
to write on the board,
I'd steal looks over to their desks
and go through my daily ritual
of deciding which one I'd choose,
if it came down to it:
fleet-footed Ed, muscled and Dionysian in his green cardigan,
or nimble-witted Ted, just as well-proportioned
and ambrosial in his blue turtleneck.
Ed or Ted? Ted or Ed? Green or blue?

With forty minutes to the bell,
Miss M. was lecturing, page after handwritten page
from her notes on Homer, mythology, and the Greeks,
Greece being the birthplace of democracy
and thus a very big deal,
her face flushing with emotion
to match her lipstick and fingernails,
and her voice almost breathless
as she spoke of Penelope's twenty-year fidelity.

Watching those ruby lips move in front of us,
I couldn't help but wonder
if they'd been kissed,
if she had her own Adonis,
who, impatient, adoring,
would fling her books
and (our) neatly corrected essays
across the room, remove her glasses,
take her in his arms,
and whisper,
Helen, forget the Greeks.
They're ancient history,
and what counts for us is now.

As the room emptied for the day,
I glanced back,
saw her erasing the blackboard,
and sent a small prayer to the gods of Olympus
that Miss M. would find true love,
that we weren't her whole life,
that her face would launch
at least one ship.

First time

There was a strong possibility it might not have happened.
This good American girl was not going to get into
Trouble
So used to saying No
Mostly to herself
No I'm not like the others
No I'm not easy
No I'm not taking the risk
No I'm not going all the way

So how did he do it
This man who'd been drafted
Three years in Nam
Now back in school on the GI Bill
Older than the rest of us
Experienced

He waited for me
Wanted me
Would have lived with me
Would not have married me
Wore away my resistance
Wooed every day every night

He showed up in my life just in time to
Teach me
Hold me
Undress me
Excite me
Calm me

And then one night he said
No more waiting

I said no I'm too nervous
I said no I'm a virgin
I said no I'm scared
I said no I'm not ready

He said
He was scared too
Nervous too
Because
He'd never been with a virgin

So you see he said
For both of us
It'll be the first time.

Strawberry trauma

Shortcake doesn't tempt him, nor does jam.
You see, he wanted to play Little League
with the other boys when school was out,
but June required a different type of exercise,

bending over, kneeling, squatting,
getting all sweaty in the acreage
where he worked beside his older brother,
who was slow and ate too many.

He however was agile and moved quickly down the rows,
refusing to think of his friends on Cedar Falls Plumbing,
who'd be chasing fly balls, learning to bunt, sliding into bases,
trading cards, checking the stats for Fox and Aparicio,

staying focused instead on the money his dad would pay
—7 ½ cents a quart, his all-time record being 72 quarts—
almost like picking coins right from the ground, he thought,
calculating over and over his possible take for the day.

Maybe the coach would still let him start,
even though he'd missed so much practice,
or maybe next year his dad would relent.
Go play ball, boy, he'd say, *you've earned the chance.*

I'm tempted to psychoanalyze, to dig deeper,
but he'll have nothing of it.
I just don't care for the taste, he says.
They never really appealed to me. Too tart.

Nina got all the calls

on the phone in the hall
of our women's dorm back in '67.
There were twelve of us on the floor,
but only one was in demand.

Nina, it's for you.
N I I I I I I NA, some guy for you.
Nina's not here, can I take a message?

My roommate Debbie and I
waited for calls that never came,
or if they did, the line would have been busy,
since Nina, wearing another of her silky nightgowns,
her auburn mane in large curlers,
would hold court draped across the stuffed throne
situated directly across from our room,

so even if our door was closed
we could hear her voice tinkling
in tones I'd never used,
and we couldn't help but eavesdrop
as she refused most dates
—skilled at letting the admirers down easy—
and accepted a few
—skilled at not seeming too eager—
all the while we crammed for tests,
planned empty weekends, tried to sleep.

When my cell rings today
I know it's for me,
such a treat
to answer calls
that are never ever for Nina.

When I didn't become a mother

What we know for sure is that
when motherhood happens

there's a beginning,
a moment of conception that's absolute
some say miraculous
a joining of two separates into one
in that explicit instant
when new life begins

followed by a period of gestation
growth and nourishment
high anticipation and wondrous expectation
vigilant preparation for the still unknown

then a shorter stage of laboring
the push to be two again
the crying out
the ultimate realization of what is
about to emerge

and finally
the defined moment of
release.

The process is scientific,
chronological,
and sequential.

There are precise dates
and occasions of celebration:
birthdays,
first steps, first lost tooth, first day of school,
christenings, quinceañeras, and bas mitzvahs,
graduations and weddings.

Looking back, you can say things like:

When I became a mother...
...I first began to know what love really is, or
...I found my highest purpose in life, or
...I understood what it meant to be a woman, or
...I would never again be able to imagine myself
                    without the joy of children.

But I didn't become a mother.
Looking back, I don't see anything linear or specific.
I have no idea of the time, or the place.
I can't point to decisions or milestones.
There are no photos framed on the wall or stored in my phone.
No memories of it stand out.

A long unhappening,
you might say,
without events or dates
to let you know
when it didn't occur.

How does one celebrate that?

Mothers and others

My mobile home

There's a photo of her in late pregnancy
standing out in our yard, in flats,
leaning slightly back on her heels,
her ankles swollen,
her extended hands placed gingerly around her belly,
wearing one of those cotton maternity dresses
that fluttered like sheets on a clothesline.

I realize that I (pre-I) am also in the photo,
contained within that stomach,
more precisely, that uterus—
called, in Vietnamese, a *children's palace*—
where for the first three seasons of life
this little amniotic princess
was sheltered and cared for
by an umbilical lady-in-waiting—
from early April through summer and fall
to late December 1949.

She tells me it was bitter cold that week
between Christmas and New Year's.
Dad drove her to the hospital Wednesday evening
and then went home to wait.

Because of the holidays
there were hardly any other patients,
it was snowing,
we were both ready,
the hospital was quiet,
even today I love snow and quiet,
and at 4 :18 a.m. on the 28th I appeared, a girl,
eager to be released,

to stretch my arms and legs
to move and keep moving
from a young age

beyond my mother's world
of imposed domesticity
and suburban enclosure

my long voyage out—
pilgrimages into books
and foreign languages
into borderlands

a mobile life
to the Berlin Wall
the Great Wall
the Wailing Wall

mostly cut off from mother
leaving her behind
fretful, cautioning, waiting, wishing
me home.

I've resisted,
and yet when I glance at her stomach,
like today, I think back to the time
when we went everywhere together
and remind myself
not to kick too hard.

Between us

It's your mother.
If you're there, pick up.
Where are you so late? Call me back,
doesn't matter what time. And don't text. (Beep.)

I hope I can stay awake. But what's the use?
Even when we talk, we're not talking.
So many things you never told me
I was dying to ask
don't ask your father said
how many times have we been through this
I can still hear him our very own Eric Sevareid
just get off her back wouldya she needs her privacy
privacy schmivacy
what's the big deal I ask you
what was so secret to keep from your own mother?
your father rest in peace he'd say *she'll tell you*
what she wants you to know when she's ready
but you didn't tell me bupkis
a clam could learn from you
so serious you were with the books such a studier
you could've had some dates some fun
that one boy he liked you what was him name—Jacob—
Jacob Steiner that's it remember him
his picture was in the paper a while ago
a doctor at Sinai you would've been on easy street
but, no, all those years living by yourself
working so hard work work work
schleppin' all over the country for what
a better job more work
lucky you got lucky that's for sure with Gregory
a decent earner a mensch even though he's not one of us
but then what happened no children not even one
no family of your own oy what happened
don't go near it, he said,
you have to leave her alone, fershtay?

40

now that he's gone
we could have a real talk a heart to heart
your father he'd turn over in his grave
but what do men know they don't talk
only about who robbed a base or invested a stock
you'd understand me if you were a mother
the hardest job ever invented
all I went through raising a family
and to be lonely now at my age vey iz mir
but what could I have done
back then we didn't really have choices
we got married all of us so young without a penny
then you came along you and your brothers
actually I was a bright girl
maybe I never mentioned there was this one teacher
back in high school he said I had—
I remember his exact words—a gift for numbers
but what's the point thinking about that now.

Hi sweetheart it's me again your mother.
Ignore my message from before. I have a headache,
I'm going to bed.
We'll talk soon. (Beep.)

Thirteen ways of looking at mother birds

~after Wallace Stevens

I.

A mother and daughter are one.
Two daughters and a mother are one.
A mother and son can be one, or two.

II.

You need a mother.
After which a mother needs you.
Etcetera.
This is a cautionary tale.

III.

The umbilical cord must be cut
Once at birth
And later once again
And then again
Etcetera.

IV.

Mothers are our destiny.
They push you from the nest
And though you may fly to distant places
For extended periods
You're not free.

V.

Among twenty snowy mountains
The only thing moving
Was the eagle eye of the mother.

VI.

I was of three minds.
Like at a Thanksgiving dinner
Where three generations of mothers
Disagree on recipes.

VII.
I do not know which to prefer.
The closeness of a mother's touch.
The beauty of *Hush little baby*.
Or the memory.

VIII.
The mother birds whirled in the autumn sky.
They still know how to catch the wind.
No one is watching.

IX.
Icicles and frost filled the window.
The shadows of mothers
Crossed it, to and fro, busy creatures.
The mood
Approaching desperation.

X.
I know foreign songs
And tempting cadences of other continents.
But I know, too,
That the mother bird will caw
Unbidden.

XI.
The river is moving.
The mothers must be flying.

XII.
It was evening all afternoon.
It was drizzling
And it was going to pour.
The mother bird perched uneasily
Wanting to go inside.

XIII.
When the mother bird flew out of sight
And could no longer be spotted
You kept scanning the sky
Despite yourself.

God helps grandmothers who help themselves

My grandma Anna typed and took dictation
for forty years in pencil skirts and high heels,
received her plaque and bikini-sized pension,
and moved to Miami Beach,
leaving winter heating bills behind
and joining a migration of senior citizens
who lived on the margins.

She took with her an ample cache of paper,
pens, typewriter ribbons, envelopes, and erasers
accumulated from her places of employment,
her unmatched stack of towels came
courtesy of Howard Johnson and Travelodge,
and her toasters, waffle irons, and blenders
had been easily procured by opening bank accounts.

When she ate lunch once a month at Flamingo's,
the local buffet, she'd bring along her own sizable
doggie bag, filling it casually with the entire contents
of the bread basket, the bread basket itself,
rolls of toilet paper and bars of soap,
handfuls of Lipton tea bags, salt and pepper shakers,
and enough packets of sugar to sweeten Biscayne Bay.

Anna made her own way,
never asking for anything,
just taking what she needed,
surviving on her wits
and her gnarly five-finger discount.

Aunt Rose

Eyelashes flirting from across our
cold Sunday oatmeal,
the scent of hairspray in the air,
those cheeks in an imperishable blush,
that skin like the ads in *Vogue* or *Good Housekeeping*,
and those perfect petal lips in showy shades,

meaning that once again she'd made us all wait
to use the bathroom, keeping the door locked
for an unfairly long time, ignoring our knocks,
emerging finally as if the cameras were waiting.
Even Uncle Robert thought she went too far,
saying that make-up was her religion.

I don't know that we ever really talked,
she and I, she wasn't my favorite relative,
too beautiful to get close to,
a Paramus Elizabeth Taylor who didn't really belong
in our JCPenny split-level family.

I wouldn't have given Rose further thought
had I not learned, in talking with her daughter
after her funeral, about her life
pre-wife, pre-mother, pre-aunt.

She'd grown up poor, that much I already knew,
in mid-Depression, and her father, Elias,
a drinker and gambler, had left for good.
I remembered vaguely that she had worked
for a time in a typing pool,
helping her mother with the bills
and her brother with his college tuition
before marrying her first boyfriend,
dashing door-to-door salesman Robert.

But it seems she had felt a different passion—
painting. Painting?
That wasn't the aunt I knew. *Oh, but yes,*
she was gifted, my mother was,
she wanted desperately to study,
to become an artist.

And so now I can't help but wonder
if that door we were knocking on
was not just to a room
with a toilet and shower
but for Aunt Rose to a private space
where she could be with

her brushes and tubes
her pencils, wands, and liners
her palette of colors
and her imagination

dabbing and mixing
applying, smoothing, and blending
daily
using her face
as her canvas.

Elias

Yesterday I went to a memorial service
for a man whose three adult children
spoke about how he didn't make a fuss,
just wrapped up his affairs,
I have to play the hand I was dealt,
this particular hand being
one of a retirement cut short,
the diagnosis of pancreatic cancer
coming three months into his new life,
begun at 61.

My father Powell was different.
Twenty-two years into retirement,
he refused to play his hand,
wanting a new one,
undergoing seven surgeries,
spitting curses and blood,
braving pain beyond even his capacity,
pitting himself against Death
and intending to win.

Powell was, it seems, unfinished,
wrestling
with his own father,
who walked out on the family
in mid-Depression, abandoning
his only son at ten years old
for drink and the track,

blue-eyed Elias who, in a photo
tucked into the back of an album,
stares coolly at the camera, his expensive hat
cocked to one side, a careless disappointer
who failed even to show up at the dock
to see his son off to war and left unanswered
the letters sent to him from many ports.

The funny thing is that I can't recall
Powell ever mentioning him.
It seemed he didn't exist
all those years,
my dad simply being
fatherless

until the end, when Elias came back
to cause trouble again, there
in the room, with us, a disturbing presence,
still uncaring, good-for-nothing.

So my father died
unbathed
unresolved
undignified
handing down
more than one generation
of accumulated damage
and aftershocks.

Aunt Edith

Even into her eighties
she loved to talk about Seattle,
the visit she and Uncle Charles had made
on their honeymoon, before the kids came along,

on the train all the way from Long Island,
where she lived in a neat bungalow
with a weeping willow in the back yard
and worked for the Red Cross—
one of those who wore a white uniform and cap,
made beds with ironed sheets and straight corners.

Her dream was to travel after retirement,
to get a passport and tour London, or Rome,
to see the Redwoods and Old Faithful,
and most of all to revisit Seattle,
to walk once more on those steep streets
rising above the blue of panoramic Puget Sound,
the views captured on their first Brownie,
bought especially for the trip.

She'd try to find that restaurant again,
the one in Pike Place Market where they served
the world's best chowder—and salmon,
oh she could still taste it, her very first salmon.
The Space Needle wasn't there in those days,
she'd plan to see it this time for sure,
to go to the top.

But Charles got crippling arthritis,
so she cared for him, stayed with him,
nursed him for twenty-five years,
and when family talk turned to the many trips
we had all taken—to Paris, Jerusalem, Tokyo—
she'd remind us that she too had traveled,
to Seattle.

Stranger danger

My offer of an old tennis ball
on the city courts is refused
by the little guy watching us play.
He reaches for it,
then hesitates and runs away.

These days in the grocery store line I don't
ask toddlers how old they are,
admire their sneakers with blinking lights,
make mention of their stick-on tattoos.

And wacky husband Phil no longer does
his Donald Duck voice,
even in airport lounges
when boarding time is delayed
and babies are howling,
it's better than a pacifier,
could calm an entire nursery,
but he resists.

It takes a village, they say,
all those aunties and uncles not by birth, but by choice,
like the gentleman who approached me
when I, maybe six years old, was wandering the streets,
having been lost for a long time on the way home
from the library in my granny's neighborhood.

I knew the address was 4828 Chalgrove Avenue,
I just couldn't find it,
so he gave me a kleenex and a glass of water,
then took my hand and walked me there.

Dishwasher

We don't need to buy a dishwasher,
my father-in-law said, *we already have one,*
glancing up during the commercial
and pointing in her direction
from his Lazy Boy as she cleared the table.

This was his anchored evening location
except when dinner was served,
always at 6 o'clock sharp.
If she wasn't quite ready, or anyone dawdled,
there would be tears.

What could they have done,
they were kids, not heroes,
just waiting to grow up, to escape,
five of them leaving mom behind
and hoping that after he retired
he might wash a dish or two himself
or learn to compliment her cooking,
three meals a day, homemade,
even the ice cream, her own recipes,

everything done just the way he liked it,
except for the time
when she came home from the hospital
after a mild stroke
and forgot to add celery
to her famous potato salad,
and he pushed it away.
It's mushy.

They were all there at the table,
having traveled back home to see her,
to spend some time and cheer her up.
I said IT'S MUSHY,
You might as well THROW IT AWAY.

And for once
they stood up for her,
asserting in five-part harmony
that the potato salad tasted
fine, just FINE. They *LIKED IT* this way,
would all want seconds.
It didn't need celery,
they shook their heads in unison,
not in the least.

But, they allowed,
motioning toward the kitchen,
don't let us stop you,
if you really need the damn celery,
go right ahead,
it's in the crisper
at the bottom of the fridge.
Please help yourself.

My Shakespeare uncle

My mom said that as a kid he'd save up
his allowance to buy LP records of the plays,
then disappear into his room.
No one could coax him out,
not for dinner, not for Boy Scouts.
He never learned to throw a ball.

To me he was Uncle Earl, or Unc,
a tall tweedy professor who puffed
on his pipe, amused himself with puns,
and gave me books I didn't want to read,
like *Shakespeare for Children*.

Once, desperate, I asked him for help
with a high school paper on tragedy
in *A Streetcar Named Desire*,
on which (he and) I got an "A."

When he developed lung cancer
and was given three months to live,
I wanted to fly out to see him,
but he asked that I simply call,
afternoons, when he would have strength.
Our talks were strained—hard not to
keep coming back to doctors, treatments, hospitals.
He was morose, unable to concentrate.

Then one day I confessed I'd never read
Othello. His curtain went up.
I began, and so began my chance to know
my uncle. He brightened and forgot his pain,
ready to explore once again
why Desdemona is drawn fatally to the Moor,
why Iago is compelled to destroy him,
why Othello could not put his suspicions to rest.

Next was *Lear,* the play young Unc chose
for his thesis topic half a century ago,
when he was still *a master of his time,*
when three months meant nothing more
than the coming season. The king,
then a subject of inquiry,
was now a companion facing final loss.

Earl's mother tongue was Shakespeare.
A thousand pages of *The Complete Works*
were in his head, in the cells of his brain,
while the cells of his body were leaving the stage.

When I asked if we could read *The Merchant of Venice*
next, he suggested we take a break.
With that, my Shakespeare uncle was gone.

The heavens themselves . . . did not *blaze forth*
his death, for he was obscure, not a prince,
and yet—in my sky—comets were seen then
and afterward.

Little boy goes out to meet the ocean

Or is it the reverse?
Could it not be that the sea,
looking for sport,
draws the little guy in toward it
the bubbly foam
    retreating   teasing   receding farther
                      he chases it   a race
his feet leaving no visible trace on the hard sand,

tinier now, alone,
he faces the ocean, pauses,
      and then, like every other time, whoa!
the water comes in again, fast,

with a mini-crash,
sending him scurrying back to shore,
barely ahead of it,
his green shorts a blur of
                    hurryhurry

his arms tiny propellers,
whoops the wave catches him,
              tosses him about
                    head under
    he scrambles up
              runs some more, shrieking

he loves this game of yo-yo,
plays it again and again,
run out, wait, turn around, run back, get wet, shriek, repeat,

he doesn't notice the cold,
the salt water he swallows,
we don't see any parents,
but they must be nearby,

or a lifeguard,
we continue watching
just in case,
just in case the ocean tires of the tame game
or forgets that he's only a little boy.

Elsewhere and back

Spawning

Only because our visitors wanted to see
salmon spawning,
we drove the three hours to Oxbow State Park,
not knowing what to expect,
and trailed behind a volunteer guide
to a spot on the Sandy River
where we waited and watched.

Before long she was there,
a lone Chinook,
swimming slowly,
returning home from the Pacific,
my god, a submarine! someone whispered.

She was barely moving,
oceans of miles behind her.
Can she detect our presence?
Does she need privacy?
But my concern was forgotten when

she came to life and began to
spawn:
turning first
on her side, then
beating
her body
repeatedly
against the river bottom—
berserk—
battering her only possession
slapping again and again
using her tail as a shovel
to scoop out gravel below
into the shape of a nest.

Back at the parking lot
we learned from our guide that
she'll finish the nest, or *redd*,
then expend her remaining strength
to lay her eggs and,
once they're fertilized by the male,
to push bits of rock over them—
as was all once done for her in this very place—
before drifting downstream to die.

We humans dream of such things,
of setting out on a long journey
and returning at the end to our origins,
of knowing our role
and fulfilling our destiny,

of perfecting the circle by
leaping the rapids
flapping our fins
and slamming our bodies
against the bottom of a river
to protect the future
beneath a bed of rocks.

Christmas Eve flight

Settled into my window seat on American Airlines 94
from New York to Tel Aviv, I receive a headset,
a newspaper, and menus for two meals
from a flight attendant wearing a Santa hat.
Somewhere high above the ocean
I turn to the obituary pages, where

a beleaguered ship, the *SS Exodus*, sags in the water—
its passengers standing close together on the decks,
holding onto the railings, peering ahead.
We're taken back to July, 1947,
when Yitzhak "Ike" Ahronovitch, age 23,
assumed the helm and sailed to southern France
to pick up refugees—mostly Jewish survivors of the Holocaust—
for transport to safe haven in Palestine,
then under British control.

I imagine myself as one of those on board,
possessing no documents, no rights,
summoning hope for another chance,
maybe even for a home,
now having spent an anxious week at sea,
then sighting hills—it's the coast of Haifa,
yes, it's really Palestine—rejoicing at having lived
to see it, to reach safety, to arrive.

As we near land,
it's as if our eyes are deceiving us,
British Navy ships in a blockade,
we're being intercepted, turned away,
and when our captain tries to break through,
two ships ram us, then British sailors try to board,
we're not equipped to fight,
but for several hours we fend them off
hand to hand— spraying fuel oil, throwing life rafts at them—
until they open fire.

Wrapped in blankets, most of my fellow passengers
are fitfully asleep.

All the refugees, the paper recounts,
more than 4,500, were taken into custody,
deported to France, then held captive
in prison-like camps in Germany.
The *Exodus*, moored off Haifa, lay derelict
for some years, and was eventually scrapped.

Things have changed since then, I remind myself,
There's a place to go, if we ever need it.
There's even a Law of Return:
Every Jew has the right to immigrate to Israel.

It's midnight, we're still hours from
the coast of Israel, and the airline crew
brings complimentary champagne
to those of us who are awake.
Merry Christmas, they toast,
and I raise my glass silently to
Captain Yitzhak "Ike" Ahronovitch.

Western ("Wailing") Wall

This first morning in Jerusalem
I enter the vast plaza
see the Wall some distance ahead of me
higher than I had imagined
so high and white against the bluest sky
and I feel in my pocket
for the folded slip of paper
I had written the night before
my prayer
that by custom
I'll leave in a crack in the wall
of this surviving place
where so many Jews before me have stood
allowing their sorrow to flow
into the ancient stones.

I'm here, but not yet ready,
so I breathe, pause, and then approach
the soaring shelter
sensing its power
I'm in its embrace
when suddenly I'm startled:
by a man heading: straight at me:
gesticulating: blocking my way:
directing me to: Stop:
saying: Not allowed.

What's wrong? Excuse me,
I don't understand.
What rules?
Where are you pointing?
Over to the right,
there's an area for women?

I walk around a long cheap-looking barrier
to reach a small section of the wall,
partitioned off from the men's territory,
you can't see over it,
there's a crush of women,
even so I join them,

it's confined, airless here, not like what I saw
on the other side, open, an oasis of sorts
where you can touch the wall,
stand with some privacy,
linger.

As more women arrive, we're pressed in together
under the unfriendly sun, unable to move,
and I begin to perspire, to burn.

I close my eyes and see—

the two Afghan girls who defied threats
meant to prevent them from attending school,
and who were blinded in an acid attack
as they walked one day to class

women forced to cover their bodies in suffocating
black and look at the world through mesh

daughters sold into lives of flickering neon and dim hope

poorly ventilated rooms in Beijing and New York
filled with teenage seamstresses huddled over jeans
from 6 a.m. to midnight, unable to keep their eyes open.

I rewrite my prayer for women who are
kept down, kept apart, kept without,
and wait my turn at this place of wailing.

Vermont Country Store Catalog

Like a fairy tale, a mail-order catalog takes you away,
in this case to a place of eternal fall,
the cover showing a plaid-shirted farmer
atop his spotless tractor,
pulling his harvest of perfect
plump pumpkins past approving cows.

Wanting to be part of the scene,
I open to the first page,
and now it's accomplished, I'm there,
it's the syrup that does it,
Fall In Love With Vermont Maple,
they urge, and I can taste it,
I'm serving up buttermilk pancakes
from the griddle and watching
the liquid gold as it drizzles
onto each stack, taking its sweet time.
I long for that breakfast,
for that old-fashioned kitchen,
where my pantry is filled with jars
of my canned pickles and homemade jams,
and where ginger spice cookies
are always baking in the oven.

Turning the pages, I picture myself
raking leaves in my corduroy barn jacket
while my mittened children
and exuberant dog leap
into the multicolored piles.
I'll cure my ailments with natural remedies,
take steamy baths with triple-milled soap,
rock by the fire as I knit and darn—
my feet cozy in hand-sewn moccasins—
and sleep in my flannel nightgown
decorated with geese in flight.

I could order all this from a catalog,
beginning with the syrup, $19.95 a pint,
free shipping, my credit card is ready,
I'm on hold, then it hits me.
I'm pre-diabetic, so no to the syrup.
I'd feel silly in moccasins, and flannel makes me sweat.

I hang up quickly, saved.
The catalog gets recycled,
I receive way too many
and can only keep a few, like the one
from Charleston Gardens,
now there's something special,
on every page a dream come true,
exquisite outdoor spaces in a land of eternal spring,
I close my eyes, and oh

how I want to be there
lounging on white wicker furniture
sipping mint iced tea
and gazing out
at my arbors and gazebos
my trellises and topiaries
the alluring scent of magnolia all around
as Carolina wrens splash
in my cherub birdbath.

French

C'est la salle à manger, he shouts,
a small boy with mediterranean skin and bristly hair,
as he skips around the table
set permanently for fourteen
with the artist's blue and yellow dishes.

Et le chat, le chat blanc, il est là!
the others rushing over to see,
they all knew about Monet's white porcelain cat,
curled up on its pedestal all these years,
not to be petted, *attention, ne touchez pas*,
a teacher in a hijab gently warns.

In the adjoining kitchen a delicate girl,
maybe Vietnamese, with wishbone arms,
sketches the row of polished copper saucepans
that hangs all along the wall.
Her classmate, a perfect braid flowing down her back
like woven ink, waits nearby, smiles at me,
her charcoal eyes taking everything in.
India, I'd guess, or Pakistan.

They're from the banlieues, my friend Christiane says
in a low voice—the districts outside Paris
where immigrants live, those places in the news
where riots start, where you can hear Arabic and Farsi,
buy prayer rugs and get good couscous.

We see them again later in the gardens,
counting the water lilies in bloom,
leaning over to see the koi,
posing for a group photo on the Japanese bridge,
children on their field trip
just an hour away
from the impoverished neighborhoods
of the *banlieue*s to Giverny

where they learn
to recognize the master's work

learn
to pronounce *nymphéas* correctly
and to love Impressionism

learn
about the art and history
of their country

learn
to be French.

My destination

Two hours' drive exactly,
I can make it, a stop halfway
at Dairy Queen for a clean bathroom
and a hot tea,
then across the coast range,
protected by sentinel Douglas firs
on both sides of the road,
I remember to breathe mountain air
through the partly opened window,
I can make it

just a few more miles—south on highway 101
to the Cannon Beach exit,
to the water,
a quick check-in at Land's End Motel,
my favorite room 55, facing the ocean,
they know me here, *welcome back*, they say,
we may have a break in the rain.

I take an apple from the basket,
a *USA Today* and *Pelican Post*,
deposit my suitcase in the room
and head just around the corner
to Lazy Susan Cafe, they know me here,
good to see you again, they say,
would you like your corner table,
they ask already knowing the answer,
and the hot seafood salad?

Fortified, I start my long walk
down the beach
moving my legs
finding my stride
taking in breath
after breath

walking
on firm sand
close to the shoreline
to Haystack Rock
my touchstone
with its three Needles
rising up high beside it
here are three things
I can never lose.

The sun comes out
for my sake
the wind calms down for me
the waves lap playfully.

Now back in my room
with the sliding door opened wide
onto the sea

I lie down and wait for the gulls

small white kites in effortless flight
on currents of air

lulling, calling.

They know me here.

Play on, words

You

They're confused.
Why are there two ways to say "you"?
the students in beginning French want to know.
Isn't "you" "you"?

Well, yes and no, I respond.
Imagine you live for a time in Paris, or Montreal.
An entire city defines your place.
Are you (vous) lost?
Do you (vous) always wear shorts in winter?
Do you (vous) know the bistro Crazy Little Pig?

Then one day a person you really like,
with whom you've become close,
who sees you as a friend,
will suggest that you use *tu*—
that you *tutoyer* each other
instead of *vouvoyer*-ing.

Say *tutoyer* twice fast, I tell the students,
and you'll sound like a songbird.

The move to *tu*, I continue,
is like entering a summer garden.
Your words are in bloom,
your sentences entwine,
the simplest phrase is fragrant.

The class listens.
As they shuffle out the door,
I think of a different *tu*,
the one voiced as you awaken
beside your new beloved.
Comment vas-tu, ma cherie?

Interrupted by the sounds of the next class arriving,
I realize I was too hard on the *vous*.
It's not standoffish or cold,
not just a starting place on the way to *tu*.

How to explain this to a generation of young people
who lead t-shirted, flip-flop lives,
wear cutoffs to class and baseball caps indoors,
call professors by their first names,
and befriend others with a click on a screen.

I'd like for them to appreciate the value
of a properly attired guardian who
stands watch at their polite—but latched— gate,
who assists them in saying:
Thank you but I have a previous engagement tonight.
That's kind of you but I'm afraid I must decline.

Why I don't check books out from the library

It's a compulsion, this underlining,
the inability to read without a pencil,
my need to make a quick horizontal statement:

This got my attention!
This is too good simply to continue on!
This needs to be remembered!

Like when Sharon Olds describes childhood
as *a long wish to be elsewhere,*
she doesn't warn you, announce in any way what's coming,

no, her words just reside there for you to see, find, notice,
not underlining themselves, asking for your approval,
and how would you show it anyway,

you're alone in your room, it's quiet, and if you applaud,
stand up and wave your arms, yell and cheer,
you'd just get tired, hoarse,

but, still, wanting to mark the occasion somehow,
you could take Anne Sexton's advice to
break crystal glasses in celebration,

or—you might save the crystal and join me
in something more extravagant

putting down the prudent pencil
and forsaking the mild underlines

in favor of spontaneous, uncensored, even outrageous
comments, scribbles, doodles, jottings, drawings, dog ears (!)

finding yourself in the company of
Poe, Melville, Plath, and Twain *sounds like a law firm*

all of whom covered pages promiscuously
such that the original text was made more important

by their marginalia, their act of dialogue
a grand conversation on a piece of paper

whoops!

n
one that you, my distiguished reader, and I can partake of
even though we may not know each other in person

we can still meet this way
we can share the page.

Ghastly

When a Brit says *ghastly*, as in
Simon and I couldn't go for our stroll in the park,
not even with our brollies,
that's how ghastly the weather was,
stretching out that first syllable,
ghaaastly,

you can't help but *laaaugh*
and think of other examples,
like peasants suffering from ghaaastly skin diseases
at the time of the plague,
with boils, sores, and pus,

or my experience at a ghastly evening lecture
on *The Regicides and Charles I*
in a roomful of pompous pontificators,
mostly portly and balding,

which reminds me of something that makes me glum,
my husband's going bald,
he's glum about it too,
but when you say *glum*, you can't really stay glum,
I'm feeling rather glum today,
see what I mean?

It's just that I miss his soft golden strands,
tassels of Iowa corn,
though if I think about it
I realize with relief
he's just losing his hair
not his head,
like poor Charles upon the scaffold,
whose ghastly end was no laughing matter.

Ode to a sardine

Oh oily little fish
so high in omega-3s
we sing to you

and vow
to picture you anew
in waters aquamarine

moving collectively
amidst thousands
in unerring synchronicity

swimming as one
in silvery choreography
unknown to science how you navigate

never shoving or bumping others
as we do in a subway, clumsily,
then unkindly evoking your name

mentioning you only then
when we're crowded, sweaty,
unable to breathe, to escape

no, no, how demeaning
to reduce a sardine
to this one claustrophobic metaphor

that has little to do
with the essence of you.
Consider yourself redeemed.

Lola's new man

He's not much, she admitted,
in the brains department,
but—and she gave me one of those smiles—
he makes up for it
in the looks department.

Lola was good at what you might call
the pigeonholing department, her mind,
as I imagined it, an old-fashioned mailroom
where each letter is slotted into its proper place.

Her older brother Harry?
Oh, lord, she'd say, he needs help
in the personality department.

The Bible? From what I remember,
she said, it always bogs down
in the begat department.

And her son Rusty, 28,
still living happily at home,
playing Metallica at all hours,
needed another shove, she avowed,
in the apartment department.

It was all just good fun with Lola
until one day she looked me over
and mentioned that
I might be amplifying a bit
in the weight department.

At which point, I debated
whether to extend her

my personal invitation
to the tact department,
or maybe just ask her to
depart from her departments.

Ish

I've loosened up now that I'm 60ish,
telling my good friend Trish I'll arrive at 5ish.
Punctuality causes anguish.

So does the let's-slim-down wish.
I'm finished with diets, all of them
keeping us famished, undernourished.
If anyone wants to know,
I weigh 140ish
and calorie non-attentiveness
is something I relish.

So, if you're with me on this, let's meet
soonish at noonish
have a longish talk
over a lavish meal
or a less foolish
and more nutritious fish dish,
we'll be replenished.

Astonishing what you can accomplish
by adding three little letters to your life,
making so much pressure, worry, stress

simply vanish.

Borrowing a word from another language

Inshallah
God willing
Allah willing
Fate willing.

A philosophy of life
A softening
A nod to the unknown
Not just for the faithful.

Humility
Expressed daily
Linguistically.

A gift from the Arabic
That I often attach to
The end of my own sentences
Mostly not aloud.

It will work out fine
It will be all right
If the stars align
If I'm fortunate
If circumstances allow
If luck is with me
Luck willing
Inshallah.

First person, singular

I

is too high

let's fix it

i think
i love
therefore
i am

much better

this i not nearly as IndIvidualIstIc
no longer being
capital, first, or singular
now definitely more inclusive
infinitely more likable

with its little
dot
at the top

limiting it
reminding it
that there are other
pronouns.

The umlaut

Two dots on top of a vowel
like in *küssen*

to pronounce it
just put your lips in a kiss
puckery

leaving a little circle
in the middle

now with your lips still protruding
say *küssen*

and then wait for the next
umlaut
to come along.

Typo hound

Used to be—
I could catch
just about every one.

I'd sense them,
smell them, hunt them out.
They didn't have a chance.

Let's take punctuation.
Errant commas were, gone in a quick dash,
(and I'd ruthlessly follow the trail
of missing quotation marks or parentheses.

Embarrassing misspelings?
No problem, I'd just use spell check
but never relay on it completely.

Inevrsions were easy
as long as you don't read for meaning.
Rather, focus on each syllable,
even pronouncing aloud: In-ver-sions.

I could give you more tips, but, truth be told,
I may no longer be the best one to offer advice.
The typos run faster than I do now—
leaving me panting in the wild chase—
or they exercise their cunning by
hiding up a tree, under leaves, beneath rocks.

This pooch has lost it's tooch.

Edickinson@gmail.com

She shared her work but Scarcely,
She'd never—Tweet or Blog!
She couldn't bear to live—Aloud
And hear the admiring Bog.

The Racket—didn't interest her,
For Fame she knew once Gained—
Could—Faithless—simply Disappear
To leave the poor—Remains.

To stay unknown—a sacred Gift!
No less than a necessity.
She trusted that this faithful path
Would lead to—Immortality.

Poetic justice

The boys' punishment, as agreed upon by prosecutor
and judge, was to spend time indoors
studying Robert Frost,
when they might otherwise
have been skateboarding, riding horses
through the Green Mountains,
or staging pranks, like the one that brought
them arrest and national attention—

breaking into a farmhouse that looked abandoned
and getting so wildly drunk
that they sullied and ransacked
what unluckily happened to be
Frost's former summer home,
an historic site filled with irreplaceable objects
and furniture, like the poet's own armchair,
now good only for firewood.

Handing out xeroxed copies of poems describing
the very Vermont territory familiar to the boys,
Frost biographer and professor Jay Parini
wasted no time letting them know
they were now in deep, dark woods.
If you're a teenager, you're always in the damned woods,
you're always facing choices.

We all know that adolescent boys are not wont
to open up, to reveal, to give words
to what may be raging inside.
One shy fellow in a baseball cap did say:
I took the wrong road.

In interviews, Parini was reluctant to speculate
on whether he or Frost had reached the boys.
A journalist couldn't help but wonder

if the lesson learned from this approach
to juvenile delinquency may have been:
I will never break into Robert Frost's home again,
or, somewhat more broadly:
I will never break into the homes of famous dead poets again.

Frost himself might well have concluded
that destruction happens quickly,
whereas education is slow,
then gone out to his porch and looked at the snow.

Some day

Musical chairs

Something about this game
seemed not fun at all, almost sad.

Whenever I played
I was left outside the circle, quite alone,
with no place to sit in comfort,
relief, or glee,
ejected from the jolly time,
how un-quick of me,
chair-less once again, not the winner,
unable to succeed in this tough
scramble,
then you appeared and offered me
your chair,

and the music began for me,
the melodies of love songs
I knew by heart,

At Last,
Some Enchanted Evening,
Only You,

so when we dance now
just you and me, quietly,
away from the crowds,
I can't help but be amazed
that sometimes great fortune
comes to those unfit to compete,
as it came that day
to me.

Limited engagements

It's the scene where they're about to elope,
Olivia de Havilland as the heiress Catherine
and Montgomery Clift as her first suitor Morris.
She waits, as do we, for him to arrive in a carriage
to rescue her from her stifling spinstered life.

Shy, plain, Catherine could never attract a man
like Morris, so her father says, her only asset
a talent for embroidery. Calling Morris a fortune hunter,
a cad, he refuses permission to marry, threatens
to disinherit her if she defies him, if she leaves.

But her father is wrong.
Her suitcase is packed,
the cobblestone streets are quiet,
Morris is on his way, just a little late,
and as she waits
the camera zooms in
on the grandfather clock
chiming through the night.

Then, as the sky begins to lighten,
she takes her suitcase one step at a time
back up
the winding stairs
in an over the shoulder shot.

I sit and stare,
unable to focus.
I'm flashing back
to when my first true love courted me,
proposed to me, my father warned me,
but I knew better, longing to marry, to escape,
then, as the date neared, my personal Morris
began to withdraw, giving no explanation.

He wouldn't have been hunting for fortune,
since there was none to be had,
he was possibly just a cad,
but I searched for the reason in the way
I dressed, wore my hair, in my dull self,
continuing all the while to believe in him,
watching the clock, the calendar,
refusing to accept that
he was gone.

The plot has moved on, with Catherine returning
at once to her life, to her embroidery,
becoming a wealthy heiress,
and getting her revenge when a remorseful Morris
reappears years later—rejecting him now in grand style—
a satisfying end, if not a happy one.

For me there was no such Hollywood script,
just a prolonged forsaken fade.

Nuptials

Wedding bells are chiming again
for Gloria, the engraved invitation has arrived,
and truly I'm happy for her,
her first marriage to Jake
having been a long mistake,
the old story, high school sweethearts,
their divorce a broken-hearted thing.

Then she found Harold, rest in peace,
a saint, that one would have lasted,
and now, finally, Mr. Right has come along
through OkCupid, she won't wear white
but wants all the rest—the rehearsal dinner,
the church, the gift registry, the cake, dinner and dancing
at the Spring Brook Country Club—
for this third forever event that means
everything to her,

but, for me, having been duly celebratory
at the first two,
I'm feeling weddinged-out.

Dear Gloria,
I'm embarrassed to have missed your wedding.
What happened is I was understudy all season
for The Marriage of Figaro and finally had my chance
to perform at the Met to a sellout crowd.

That would have been a great excuse, but the real reason,
I must admit, is the hot air balloon I was riding in
was carried off by the wind
into an Iowa sweet corn field
that was so green and tempting
we stayed as long as we could,
subsisting on juicy yellow kernels
and bedding down in the stalks.

Actually, the truth, can you ever forgive me,
is that I did it again,
somehow getting the time wrong,
and the place,
arriving in Portland, Maine,
a day too late, yet quite luckily entering a church
with my exquisite bouquet
just as another couple was walking down the aisle,
so I hope you don't mind
that the substitute bride received your flowers,
since they surely would have wilted
had I sent them on to you in Oregon.

Singing *Che gelida manina* at his bench

The *New York Times* writes the best obituaries,
like the one today about Antonio "Nino" Bianco,
a master diamond cutter who, working at his bench
in *blissful anonymity* for thirty years,
was entrusted with some of the world's
largest, rarest, and most valuable stones—
gems so important as to have names,
like *Flame*, a pear-shaped white diamond
nearly the size of a man's nose.

We're told, Signore Bianco, that your process
of *teasing luster and light from diamonds*
in *protracted courtship* could take
an entire year to consummate.
Before ever making a cut, you'd study
the rough, shapeless surface of a stone for months,
slicing and polishing tiny windows on its exterior
that let you *peer into its heart* and
discern the finished diamond gleaming within,
waiting, like Sleeping Beauty,
for you to wake it.

A *quiet eminence*, you worked in silence
but for the hum of your grinding machine.
At a certain point, however,
when you began to sing opera,
it meant that the task of transforming
a *lump of carbon . . . into a world-class diamond*
was nearly done.

The *Times* stops here, but I sip my tea
and think about your private life.
I'd like to know if you loved your wife,
Caterina, mentioned in the paper only as a survivor,
as much as your stones.

Was she a beauty from the start?
Did you respect her as you did
each crude chunk of coal? Did you tease
her? Sing to her? Feel bliss with her?
Did you wish to know her every
facet, hold her from every angle?
Was she your Flame?

E-V-R-C-E-O-R

With the right two letters on your Scrabble rack
things can be returned instantly, effortlessly
to their original state:

a toddler's knee un-skinned
an email un-sent
a reputation un-tarnished

a missile un-launched
a promise un-broken
the oil from a tanker un-spilled

unlike life outside Scrabble where
a jumbo jet can't be un-crashed
nor a fortune un-gambled away

and where the gymnast who has practiced her routine
on the balance beam over and over again
day after day to the point of perfection

only to fall off in Olympic competition
cannot un-fall
no two letters will help

unless of course she decides to retry four years later
the re- being more flexible, forgiving
than the un-

so regarding our blow-up that cannot be unblown-up
it's true I can't un-say un-scream any of those words
un-offend you un-hurt your feelings un-slam the door

But is there a chance of re-pair?
a way to re-awaken affection
re-build trust

re-gain confidence
re-kindle passion
re-commit?

That sounds
difficult—
where to start?

Happy hour at the rooftop bar?
Dinner and a concert in the city?
Homemade lasagna and Netflix?

Perhaps a friendly
game
of
Scrabble?

My whale tale

I've long been fascinated by whales,
having read half of *Moby-Dick,*
and I always take my binoculars to the coast
during migration season to spy spouts
on the whales' regular swim from Baja to Alaska.

In the past it's been the size that fascinated,
but now it's the songs, those sounds Melville,
who knew everything about whales—
the price of blubber on the market,
how to position one's harpoon,
the complexities of cetological taxonomy—
died too soon to experience.

We know today that they sing, compose,
the males, like when Phil performs solo in the shower:
Well——be-bop-a-lula she's my baby.
Be-bop-a-lula I don't mean maybe,
and I know I'm the one,
I can hear him even from downstairs
and picture him soaping up,
feeling the stream of water
from the double shower head
I bought him for his birthday,

the tunes of whales traveling much farther,
up to thousands of miles through the ocean.
You can hear them on YouTube,
see their liquid music on sonograms,
but even after a half century of study,
no one knows their purpose.

Are the males trying to attract females?
Scientists say no, since females don't seem interested,
nonetheless I consider it possible,

thinking of Phil, who has moved on to
Some enchanted evening you may see a stranger,
that's our song, so romantic,

a female would *have* to be interested.
Imagine her tuning in to
a jam session of humpbacks
engaged in some sort of rivalry
to reach the top of the charts,

she'd pay attention, knowing that her guy
is sending it out through the waves—
whistles clicks chirps—
crooning *Somewhere beyond the sea,*
She's there waitin' for me.

Altitude

my seat belt fastened
30,000 feet above the ground
when you encircled me in your arms
I did not suspect
a crash landing

New shoots

Green
visible on branches
of the weathered hydrangea
I thought I had forgotten
how to flirt

Some day

You may have to kiss a lot of princes
before you meet your frog.

It's not that I'm categorically anti-prince
some might actually be yours forever

as long as you act the part, filling your closet
with satin and sequins, with different shades of pink

always wearing your contact lenses
and never your fuzzy slippers

perfecting the wide-eyed stare of admiration
and the trick with your eyelashes, and rarely eating.

Ah, the kiss. Certainly you'll kiss him, or more precisely
let him kiss you. Just close your eyes as he draws you near

and emits his charm, allowing you to press against him
to take in the scent of his pomade.

He'll be true as long as you never complain about the days
he spends jousting and caring for his stable of white horses

while you wait at the window
wondering if this is all there is
listening—perhaps unawares—for a distant croak
dreaming of that secluded pond
where you and your Frog Charming
will hop and leap together
splashing from pad to pad.

In the shade

In the shade

Wednesday 9 a.m., late summer, 16 hot meals on wheels.
Roz steers her station wagon
in the direction of hungry people.

We ring the bell once, then again.
Jenny, 92, can hardly hear—her yappy dog alerts her.
She apologizes for being in her nightgown.
Behave Bella, she scolds, but the tiny bodyguard
doesn't listen, making sure we keep our distance.

Milly sits outside on her lawn chair,
surrounded by plastic ducks.
She spends so much time with her webbed companions,
Roz tells me afterwards, that she doesn't really mind
not having a TV. If it's too hot,
she moves the ducks into the shade.

Susan, stylish despite worn-out clothes,
mentions shyly that the paintings on the wall
are her oils. None are recent, though,
she confesses—there's no money for paint
nowadays. But, she smiles, her rheumatic fingers
might drop the brushes anyway.

A former navy man, Hal has a strong handshake.
Even hunched over his walker,
he's tall and distinguished.
He invites us to take a seat in his room
the size of a ship's cabin, his only view
the neighbor's chain-link fence.
I'd ask him about his life at sea,
but we've fallen behind,
and the meals in the trunk will get cold.

Janice is waiting for us, her table set for one.
She says her Social Security barely covers her rent any more,
but she's terrified of nursing homes,
her friend Sally just died in one.
While I look the other way, Roz separates
her meal into smaller portions—half a turkey sandwich
and an apple for now, the rest wrapped in plastic
and placed on an empty shelf of the fridge.
The next delivery is Saturday.

Now, looking back, I recall
that the stops were rushed, too short.
If only I could have stayed a while to clean and dust,
run the vacuum, open the windows,
throw out the bouquets of plastic flowers,
put away the photos of children who never visit.

And I wish there'd been time for at least
a walk around the block, or some small chats,
maybe a cup of coffee, we could have brought
a Danish or some fresh scones.

It's August again, and I really ought to call Roz
to see if she needs some help,
and to ask about the oil painter, the navy man,
the lady with the ducks, and the others
who may still be on her route.

Elephant grief

They say elephants refuse to leave
the dead body of a loved one,
trying to revive it, raise it back up,
then at some point covering it
with dirt and brush:
elephant burial.

Elephants are known to return
to the deceased for months,
even years, creating paths
through the forest
to visit the carcass
and caress it
with their trunks:
elephant memory.

A female was observed standing guard
over her stillborn baby for days,
her head and torso drooped in mourning:
maternal heartbreak.

Aisha, an orphan, six months old,
being cared for in a sanctuary,
stopped eating and died
just three weeks
after her second mother,
a human, was called away.

Elephant grief
smothers
stomps
tramples
weighs tons.

Its sounds are high-pitched
pulsing through arteries
reverberating in the vital organs
before trumpeting forth in
wild piercing vocalizations.

With legs like aged tree trunks,
it lumbers on.

Razor clams

If you want some, you'll have to clean them first,
Annie announced to her dinner guests,
they're in the cooler on the porch.

Lifting the lid, I was reminded of my 60th birthday,
when a crate arrived from Boston with two lobsters
sent *direct from the ocean to your table,*
what a treat, I thought,

until I heard scratching sounds
coming from the box,
oh my god, they're not alive,
are they? A peek inside confirmed
the company's promise of freshness
and launched an afternoon of discussion
as to how to deal with our two new friends,

Lloyd and Lilly, there was no way to spare them,
keep them as pets, we'd might as well eat them,
but it didn't seem right, I had to turn away
even before the water had reached its boiling point.

Now here we were again.
Clamming is hard work,
Annie said, showing us the long hollow tubes
you push into the sand to search out
the strange creatures that can dig
as much as four feet below the surface,
moving vertically in the same place their entire life,
little elevators going up and down never sideways.
You need a permit, you know, to clam,
and they limit the number you can take.
We could each have three.

So I broke open the first one to reveal
not a pearl, rather an oblong piece of flesh
still squirming in my hand
as I began to dissect it
with a pair of kitchen scissors,
cutting off the rubbery neck
and the muscular foot,
removing all the black parts,

and whispering to it that I'm glad,
little clam, your shell
is sharp enough
to make at least some of us pay
for what we do.

Worry

Be empty of worrying
~Rumi

it winds
itself
like a vine
around both legs

I try to cut it
prune it
but now my arms are
wrapped

and then it attacks
and binds
my heart
my mind

imagine me a mummy
swathed swaddled
enshrouded

worry wants to
bury.

Newport, Oregon

A small crowd watches as her blade sails through flesh
the length of her outstretched arm,
meeting no bones, no resistance,

the entire dorsal side from head to tail
separates, she flops the fish over,
and whoosh the ventral side is off.

A few more perfect incisions,
the prized pieces are dipped into water
and bagged, the others tossed away.

A priestess on the dock, she performs her rituals
in a slicker and boots, without prayers or blessings,
there are no mourners, no heads bowed, yet it's eerily quiet

as she lifts the next one up high by the tail,
as if to say, behold, this is a fish of God,
a full-grown Chinook that swam the ocean, proud,

and before I can fully admire it,
it's in pieces, slap, slice, flop, slice,
she wipes her brow, there are more lined up at her feet,

laid out neatly, waiting their turn
patiently, blue tags through their mouths,
beyond protest, soon to be delivered.

Yad Vashem

You can buy kosher snacks and sit a while
in the cafeteria of the Holocaust Museum—
Israel's Remembrance Center honoring
the Jewish victims and the Righteous
who risked or lost their lives to save them.

My husband and I order hummus wraps
and pomegranate juice. I'm not ready to talk,
but the couple from our tour wants to tell us
about their son on scholarship in pre-med at Purdue
and show us photos of their daughter's Bas Mitzvah.

Joking, flirting, and passing around a tattered
    Grand guide de Jérusalem,
the young adults at a nearby table,
probably on holiday from a French university,
could just as easily be enjoying themselves
in a Left Bank cafe or jazz nightclub.

The pair at the window, resembling Bergman and Bogie,
sit side by side, whispering to each other (in Italian?).
He strokes her hair, her cheek, he wears a ring.
They dip into a chocolaty dessert with two spoons,
they're at leisure, he kisses her hand, she blushes.

At a far table, an excitable lady in bright red
speaks Hebrew on her cell as if through a megaphone
and searches her purse for a lipstick,
while her daughter consumes an ice cream sundae.

All at once a class of uniformed schoolgirls
comes in, a flock of merry sparrows,
notebooks and pens in hand,
their teacher holding the door,
calling in friendly tones to the stragglers.

When our tour guide gives the signal,
we collect our things, purchase a few postcards,
and board the bus for our next stop
at Mahane Yehuda, the city's popular outdoor market.

From Palestine with love

The Berlin Wall,
built to last,
has fallen,
existing today only in photographs,
in history books,
in the memories of those
whose lives were severed
by it, whose hopes were caught up
in its barbed wire.

A museum at the old checkpoint
is dedicated to it,
lively karaoke events are held weekly
in its former *death strip*,
and you can buy
pieces of it on eBay
fashioned into
paperweights.

But barely was it down
when construction began
in the West Bank
on what is called
in Hebrew a *separation fence*,
in Arabic an *apartheid wall*.

The Israeli side is icy smooth
kept clean, antiseptic
gray slabs lined up
across the landscape
like massive gravestones
grim
guarded.
No one goes near it.

The Palestinian side is teeming,
littered with bottles and trash,
a raw public place for resistance
along a gigantic free message board
that allows people to cry out,
every reachable inch of concrete canvas covered

with larger-than-life-sized portraits of
Yasser Arafat heroic
Leila Khaled armed
Anne Frank in a keffiyeh

with scrawled slogans
some predictable: *No justice, no peace*
some historical: *Ich bin ein Berliner*
and some lighter: *Make hummus not war*

and with scribbled protests
Palestinian lives matter
All people are chosen
Fadi and Baseem want this wall TAKEN DOWN.

Two rickety yellow ladders
propped against the wall beside buckets of paint
await the return of artists working up high
on a three-dimensional man with a sledgehammer
smashing holes in the cement.

Other murals show a white dove in a bullet-proof vest,
a girl with pigtails holding colorful balloons that take her upward,
a group of boys hurling rocks, intifada-style,
at unseen goliaths on the other side,

and something smaller, you could almost miss,
depicts a masked figure aiming a slingshot
high across the Wall,
his projectile a simple red heart
inscribed: *From Palestine with love.*

Passing

My last name works in my favor, evoking
innocent picnics, wildflowers, and butterflies—
a Summerfield—
not containing any of the precious
gold or silver metals that give you away
or any Germanic *wolfs* or *steins*.
And Ellen is generic enough,
declining to announce itself
like the Leahs and Rachels of the Old Testament.

When curious people try to guess
my heritage from my looks,
they end up way off in exotic places,
in Sicily or Istanbul,
or in Greece with its turquoise beaches and olive trees,
rather than in the shtetls of peasant Russia
or the ghettoes of central Europe.

Can you blame me for passing?
I mean, what's wrong with blending in,
going unnoticed, there are *meshuggeneh* (crazy)
people out there, even the smallest mistake,
putting a menorah in your window
or wearing a Star of David around your neck,
can cause *umglick* (trouble).

I don't want to be a coward,
but I need problems like a *lokh im kopf* (a hole in the head),
so mostly I'll just keep quiet, mind my own business,
enjoying the sunshine, the fragrance, the ambience
in my God-given summer field.

Shalom.

The poverty line

When you live below it
Can you use it to hang out your clothes?

Do you wait in it for bread
And stand in it for no work?

Is it the shortest distance
Between having nothing
And going nowhere?

Can you put a worm on one end of it
And catch enough for a meal?

Can a friend throw you one
And pull you to safety?

Does it show on your face?
Is it marked on your palm?

Do you step out of it
When you protest
And get back in it when you fail?

"El sueño" ("The dream")

I'm asleep
Early morning
They're coming after me again
I have to run away
They're getting closer
But my legs refuse to move
I'm paralyzed

I wake slowly
needing a bit of time
to distinguish dream from non-dream
to know for sure that
I'm here, safe, alive

now I'm sure
and the ordeal ends
as usual
with relief

I can rise
dismiss the demonic
bury it

something Frida could not do
this woman wrapped in sleep
her face turned toward us
her bed adrift in the clouds
a peaceful scene were it not for the skeleton
lying directly above on the canopy, a bunked twin,
positioned sideways on his elbow, vigilant,

a white form with sooty tunnel eyes, no lashes or lids,
his teeth showing in an expectant grin,
a pallid bouquet held on his chest,
wires and explosives running through his bones.

She sleeps.
Frida sleeps in the bed
she inhabited, painted, enshrined.

I can imagine
that when she begins to awaken
she might wonder
if it hadn't just been a bad dream
all of it
the polio at age six
the streetcar accident
her fractured ribs, collarbone, and spine
her amputated leg
the miscarriages
the 32 surgeries
the steel corset that holds her together

just a bad dream
un mal sueño

and that for
a few uncertain moments
she might actually believe she can
shrug it off
toss aside the blanket
and walk away

as I do now
leaving my own skeleton
propped and waiting.

Los 33

On October 12, 2010, 33 men entered a mine in Copiapó Chile for another day of work

d
o
w
n

a

h
a
l
f

m
i
l
e.

When the mine collapsed they became trapped with no outside contact and almost no food for

1
2
3
4
5
6
7
8
9
10
11
12
13
14
15
16
17
days.

T h e n

f o o d

mini-Bibles

and letters

r e a c h e d

t h e m

in

c a p s u l e s

sent down

through

t h i n

t u b e s

a b o u t

this wide.

I won't re-

of the earth.

All returned to the surface

All 33 survived.

friends.
and
family
with
reunited
and
at the top
safety
to
brought
was
time
a
at
miner
one

miraculously

live reports and rejoiced as

us on the planet tuned in to

when more than a billion of

and the final dramatic rescue

the 69 days underground

Banderas, for details of

film, *T he* 33, with Antonio

now, or you can watch the

to read more, it's history

you can go to *Wikipedia*

count the story here,

What is it about this story that
captured our attention, inspired us,
gave us hope? Think about it, we don't
know these miners, don't care about
them. If we cared, we wouldn't have sent
them down in the first place into that

h

o

l

e

known   to   be   notoriously
unsafe. But I wasn't the one
after all who sent them down there.
I've never even been to Chile, nor do
I know, I suddenly realize, what they
were mining for. I look it up—
copper and gold. After the rescue, the
men were initially treated like rock
stars, receiving gifts, meeting with
dignitaries like Chile's president,
and appearing at Disney World wearing
yellow mining helmets with black mouse
ears. But while many people profited
from their story, the 33 have largely
been cheated and forgotten.
Most still live in poverty,
suffering from PTSD and other illnesses.
Some have returned to the mines.
The mining company was not held
responsible. A sequel to the film
would need to show that those who
work beneath the surface of the earth
and become trapped below cannot
escape the feeling even when above of being
b   u   r   i   e   d
a   l   i   v   e.

Rescue me

Looking for just the right dog to adopt,
I subscribe to alerts that pop up on the screen—

ping—

Tulip, ID #321299, was freed from a locked barn
where she rarely saw humans or daylight.

This is clearly not one of those sites where doggies speak:
Looking for a lap dog? Well, guess what? I'm looking for a lap.

She has the vacant eyes of one who has waited too long,
her fur overdue for suds and water, for a patient brush,

she's too gaunt and lifeless to please the camera,
yet it's her only chance, this one photo.

Even if she needs me, somehow I already know
I won't take Tulip, I delete her, continue my work—

ping—

it's Ruby, ID #403332, Addison's disease.
Her owners can't afford her medication,

don't want to put her down, she's dignified,
deserves a chance, but sadly I'm not the one—

ping—

petite Pierre appears, ID #760392,
a cup of cappuccino you want to pick up with both hands,

tear stains on his eyes, he's in a kill shelter,
two days left, can I save him?

I imagine his reaction when I bring him home and show him
his sunny corner outfitted with a wraparound fleece bed.

I could get him one of those rhinestone leashes
for our first walk in the neighborhood,

the application is simple, no fee for my Pierre,
thankfully he's neutered and his vaccinations are current—

ping—
Aurora pops up Rescue Me!

ping—
Bella Bee Rescue Me!

ping—
Lucky Ralph Rescue Me!

ping—

rescue

me.

Body and soul

Girls' night out

I'm invited to a Girls' Night Out,
a chance to *mingle and ask plastic surgery questions
in a relaxed atmosphere,*
hosted by a beautifully landscaped surgeon
who will reduce her fee by $500
if you schedule a procedure within a month.

So where did they get my name?
Were scouts sent to my town
in search of sags and bags?
Did they target the last hold-outs,
the ragged few protecting the aging fort
as the walls crumble all around?

Please RSVP by October 15.
Needing to read up, I begin with
the memoirs of a Park Avenue plastic surgeon
who boasts a *personal radar* that
penetrates skin,
visualizes underlying bones, muscles, and fat,
and allows him to calculate precisely how
to *reverse the cruelties of time.*

The date approaching, I feel besieged
by promises shot over my ramparts,
making it nearly impossible not to defect,
not to join the battle against epidermal variegation,
potato legs, bloat, and walkabout eyebrows.

As a last stand, I invite my best friends
for dinner and a movie—our own girls' night out—
and observe at the table around me flabby arms,
mouths heading south, extra chins, eyebrows taking a stroll.

Did anyone else get the invitation?
No? Indignant, my loyal chums
convince me to hold out.
But barely into the movie I lose track of the plot,
preoccupied with studying the actors' faces
and necks for plumping, retouching, refurbishing.

Not used to being up so late,
I fall wearily into bed,
too tired for my nightly skin care routine,
but turning to sleep on my back
rather than my side—so my right cheek
won't cave in prematurely.

Checking me out

When I ask for my senior discount
at the neighborhood grocery store—
ten percent on Wednesdays—
he looks me over, furrows his brow,
then asks for proof.

Proof? Of what, young man?
Of your bad manners?

I don't say that, though.
I scrutinize him back,
wondering if he really thinks
I would lie, for 96 cents,
and if I were lying,
is he sure he wants to expose me,
or any older lady,
in front of the others in line.
Has he thought this through?

Of course he may have expected
I'd take it as a compliment,
feeling flattered, thanking him for asking,
tossing my hair back or wetting my lips
as I flash my proof.

I sigh and search in my purse
for my driver's license, what a hassle,
you'd think we were in a big city
or something, this isn't exactly L.A., you know,
how ridiculous in a mom and pop store,
I should just call for Krista the manager,

and then I realize this fellow is new,
just trying to do his job,

no use making a fuss,
so I tell him he doesn't look old enough
to be working the cash register,
and I ask him for proof.

Hallux rigidus

Today the surgeon told me
that the joint at the base of my big toe
can hardly flex
anymore,

it's gone from *hallux limitus*
to *hallux rigidus*,

not what I wanted to hear,
neither in English nor in Latin,
which reminds me of my two years of high school Latin,
I think it was mandatory then,
but at least the teacher was not too *severus*,
dressing occasionally in a toga
to deliver speeches to the Senate,
unlike that geometry teacher with the bow-tie
who suffered from personality *rigidus maximus*,
catching even tiny errors,
ruling over you,
forcing you to deal with hypotenuses
and legs of triangles
when you just wanted to be outside
with your friends hitting balls,
running the bases.

Ah, running, will that be possible
after my operation? They'll fuse my bones
so the toe won't move at all,
to reduce the pain.

I should have asked if
I'd be able to walk without limping,
stay balanced,
wear closed-toe shoes,
but all I could think about was
running.

Will I still be able to run?
I'd miss it, even at 60,
not sprints or marathons,
just the act of running,
to catch a bus, to get out of the rain,
to chase a kite at the beach
all the way to the sky.

Acupuncture third treatment

Mr. Jian of few English words
leads me to a room with a quiet bed,
a single orchid, and some charts on the wall
showing people measled with black dots.

As I lie on my back,
he places a decorative wooden box
on my bare abdomen and ignites the herbs inside.
Closing my eyes, I feel the warmth spread
through my body while the unusual aroma
of moxa fills the room.

The needles used to porcupine me,
nine of them this week,
go in quite easily, surprisingly so,
these tiny probes,
thin as an invisible crack
in a vase from the Zhou dynasty,
penetrating my skin, or even my scalp,
with just a quick prick,

unless of course
your energy channels aren't flowing,
like when my big toes receive
one needle each, painful.

Oh, that really hurts,
what's happening, please,
Mr. Jian?

Blockage.

What's blocked?

Anger.

Anger? Really? What anger?
Like at myself for ruining the trip
to Tacoma with my mother?

No, not at self.

So I spend the hour thinking
about why I'm angry, with whom,
I breathe and look out the window
at the plum tree beginning to open up,

and the needles and box do their silent work,
allowing me to release my anger,
to let it go,
so that it
wafts and curls
and floats away
into the air
like the vanishing
smoke
of moxa.

Biological clock

If it were just a wristwatch
you could yank it off
stomp on its face
drown it in the bathtub
or place it in the path of a moving train.

A kitchen clock could be knocked
off the wall, smashed with a spatula,
left for dead without batteries.

And a grandfather clock
could be put to sleep simply by
removing a few parts.

But this invisible timepiece inside you
is of a different construction,
embedded deep in tissue, bone, and marrow.

At first its tactic seems almost friendly—
to nudge a bit
tic tic tic tic

Then, steadily,
the tempo and volume increase
as it intrudes rudely on your days
and ambushes you at night
its alarm going off
its face glaring at you
its hands striking you

an anatomical despot
that waits you out
wears you down
weakens you
with an unwavering will.

The time will come, I know,
when it will
slow   down
run   down
Die   down.
Stop.

How will it feel
I wonder
when that happens.
When it's too late to

revive it
shake it alive
detect its presence
rewind it
turn it back

when
inside me
there's no movement.
no sound.
no life.

Lost and pound

The seven pounds of flesh I've wanted to lose for so long
are finally gone, and I can't help but question where they are
exactly, those portions of myself, possessing everything—
the cells, the nerves and blood vessels, the DNA—
unique to my body, seven pounds of me,
equivalent to one of the purple weights I lift every day.

They can't just be nowhere—the Law of Conservation of Mass
clearly says that matter cannot be created or destroyed,
so I imagine my winged bundles of fat ascending
into the heavens, admitted by St. Peter
into a gilded storage unit high above,
preserved in ziplock bags, and securely tagged
with my name, date of birth, and Social Security number.

But wait. Are we to understand instead
that when the triglycerides break down
into carbon, hydrogen, and oxygen atoms
and are released into the ether,
they're now transformed,
no longer us, no longer identifiable,
unable to resume their former states?

I actually don't believe that, since experience shows
that my pounds are never permanently gone
no matter how many times I lose them,
rather they wait for me faithfully wherever they reside,
in the chocolate chip cookie dough, potato skins, birthday cake,

ready sooner or later,
with the kind assistance of St. Anthony,
to return to their former places
as if they had never left.

Clothespins

When I woke up this morning
I couldn't remember the word for *clothespin*,
not in German or French (though I once knew
Wäscheklammer and *pince à linge*),
or even in English.
Happily though it doesn't matter,
since I don't use them anymore.

Nerves of spaghetti

They train for years on the ice,
then have four minutes to show
what they can do. Triple lutz,
double toe, staying focused,
focused,
four more jumps,
three more spins,
the death spiral at the end of the program,
no room for doubts or jitters,
for losing one's nerve, the nerves
of champions being steely like the blades
of their skates.

I'm just glad it's not me
in front of those crowds,
my nerves being more spaghetti-like,
my courage going limp
in boiling water.

So thankfully my days of
throwing runners out at the plate,
auditioning for the orchestra,
sending work to publishers,
asking for raises and seeking promotions
are over,

and I've made up my mind
to keep the temperature low from now on
by refusing to compete at pickleball or even bridge,
turning down invitations to speak at Kiwanis,
passing up the chance to read at open mics,
hosting only potlucks.

But why feel bad about it,
maybe this is a time after all
to lie curled up in a bowl,
enjoying the warmth, the comfort
of my fellow noodles.

Kwan Yins in our midst

She feels for the knots in my shoulders,
probes my body for aches,
applying just the right amount of pressure,
using her strong hands, her elbows
to soften my back and neck,
to give me relief.

Fifteen minutes, thirty minutes, an hour,
my time to lie still, hers to work on me.
I thank her quickly—the next client is waiting—
not asking about her. I know she has her own woes,
but I need my strength for mine.

On my drive home, I think of statues I've seen
of Kwan Yin, the goddess of compassion,
who was so committed to understanding
the needs of others—and offering help—
that her head and hands split apart
and multiplied
so she could see in all directions
and extend one thousand hands.

When she poses, Kwan Yin is serene,
flawless,
but only because—like all healers—
she hides her personal struggles.

More truthful statues would show
that many of her hands are weary, calloused,
arthritic,
some of her fingers are
broken off,
most of her eyes are bloodshot
and, although she resists sleep,
some are closed.

Can Kwan Yin pause, lie down for an hour?
Will anyone be there to close the blinds,
fetch a blanket, bring some bandages?
Who might feel for the knots in her back and shoulders?
Who will be present to smooth her foreheads
and massage her outstretched hands?

Selfies

Background music

For some time now I've been putting on
the gentler Beethoven, his sonatas and string quartets,
in the early morning, he's there in the background,
an unobtrusive guest, sipping tea in the parlor room,

until suddenly I hear my favorite passage,
the one in his String Quartet no. 16
that's achingly slow, unearthly,
with the cello staying low, grounded,
while the violins ascend.

It's a rare bird calling from a distance.
Or a prayer the gods strain to hear.
It's the memory of someone close who is gone.

I've heard it dozens of times, but each time
I find myself needing to pause,
to close my eyes, listen, let taut muscles release.

This morning I'm emptying the dishwasher
when the section begins.
I stand still, my eyes close,
and just at that moment the sun
breaks through the Oregon clouds.
I feel it playing on my face
streaming through the kitchen window
illuminating me and the room
intensely present.

Then as the notes fade away
the sun retreats
and presently the soft rain
begins again.

The seat across

I can't stop looking at her, haute couture,
the F train graced by her presence,
I try to make out the labels—her handbag Louis Vuitton,
her scarf Hermès, her four-inch strappy heels Manolos,
a Parisian air about her, Deneuve-like,
she must be an actress, film or stage,
a face that invites staring.

I've been sitting across from her since Lexington and 63rd,
five stops, thankfully she hasn't noticed me,
my cold weather boots tucked beneath my seat,
suddenly she's standing up, moving
to the exit as if cameras are flashing,
the doors open, she steps off,

and someone else grabs her seat, a hipster,
earphones, his skateboard covered with blazing flames
that match the tattoos shooting up his neck.
I'm sure he has lots on his mind,
not easy to become a man in today's world,
he'll make his way.

I could stay here all day, warm, anonymous,
the seat across being vacated, occupied,
vacated, occupied, by people with stories
that cross mine, then uncross,

each with their entrances and exits,
playing their own leading roles,
carrying their portable fates from place to place,
offered generously to me as cameos
in a private screening that reels on.

Self-defense

For as long as I can remember
I've kept a putter under my bed
just in case I hear strange noises
and must creep out in my nightie
to wait hidden behind the door
for the ill-fated intruder
who, upon entering my room,
will be whacked into unconsciousness
(but not harmed fatally,
or even too seriously,
as would certainly occur
with a 9-iron).

A girdle by any other name

Constrains the same
Even if you call it
Shapewear by Spanx
Which makes it sexy
Somewhat naughty
And thus sells it
To a whole new generation
Of women who would never
Dream of wearing
What we wore
Or what they wore before that
Called corsets.

Cheers!

no apéritif
or digestif
no
pouring
pairing
tasting
prosting
toasting
to life
to health

no
buzz
or high
no salud
or kampai

no drinking
or clinking
no use
or abuse

no Shiraz
or Merlots
no Syrahs
or Bordeauxs

no nose or bouquet
no sommelier
no Chardonnay
or Cabernet

no sparkling rosé
or fruity frosé

today.

Wisdom

wise old onion
allowing us to
weep
freely
unashamedly
go ahead
it says
why not
have a good cry

Poser

A nude bronze reaching upward and backward,
balanced high on her toes, her spine arched so far
that her chin points straight up toward the sky,

her three dimensions being put into two
by a man crouched nearby on a collapsible stool,
a drawing board on his knees, Mr. Dwight Deworgé,
Haitian-born, educated at Juilliard,
making a living from his museum drawings,
a box of pencils and his neatly folded jacket on the floor.

Your eyes go back and forth, back and forth
from the large bronze to the piece of paper,
you keep a respectful distance, we all do,
except for two little boys, brothers it seems,
who get as close to him as they can,
leaning in to see everything,
hurling fastballs at him:
are you famous? are you almost finished?
do you make mistakes? what'd you pick her for?
is it for sale? more than five dollars?

And he seems glad to answer—
all the while continuing to work
on the neck and throat that are exposed
as far as anatomy will allow.

You can find the original in the grand vestibule
of the American Wing of the Met,
seven feet tall, holding
her pose, oblivious to the crowds,
you can walk all around her,
observe a woman's shape
lifting and reaching
beyond any imagining.

As for the drawing, it hangs on the wall
beside my bed, modeling for me
a way of being, a pose
she urges me to try.

Unruly ones
(poems that didn't fit anywhere else)

Unruly muse

you can see his idea of me in museums
worldwide where I'm displayed

in our famous red armchair
my hands folded as usual

or wearing that collared dress
and holding a flower hour after hour

hanging among the Leonardos, Rembrandts, Wyatts
with unbound hair—

in a green hat—in the conservatory—
in the garden—in blue—

with a fan—
and you'll no doubt admire his genius

it's about him
always

even when you look at me
you'll remember him

you'll talk and write
of Paul Cézanne

though I'm the one in the frames
sitting still

a still life
not moving budging shifting

statued near him for twenty years
the art of sitting perfected

Madame Cézanne
with the oval face he loved

to paint
Madame Cézanne never refusing

to be his model his muse
an honor to pose—

so you might imagine.
Now, if you look carefully,

you can find me, Marie-Hortense,
expressed twenty-nine times

in different ways
as I tell my side

and claim myself
in his portraits.

Timing

Cooking time varies
depending on the wattage of your microwave
and the precise number of kernels in the sealed bag.

Wait until popping slows
or you smell something burning.
When you can count one to three seconds
between pops,
press "Stop."

Nerve-wracking.

Press "Start."
Listen.
Nothing at first.
Then

pop

pop pop pop

Don't go away. Stay focused.

        pop   pop STOP!

How did you do?
Take a look, but don't expect perfection.

I've never timed it just right.
Either some corns will be left over,

or some will be scorched,
but no use getting worked up about it,

there are way more important things,
like when you invest your life savings in the market.

With stocks you want to buy at the low point,
just before the rally, and sell at the peak, right before a slide.

Mistakes are costly

bust   bust bust   bust bustbustbustbustbustbust

Orange

It appears selectively,
does specific jobs,
and is usually at its best in small, careful doses,

like in Florida citrus groves,
where nature's painterly dabs are interspersed
and hung like holiday ornaments from the trees.

Or when it rises atop a Bird of Paradise,
its slim sepals pointing upward,
helping the plant take flight.

Monet began an entire movement
with just the tiniest circle and a few strokes.
Impression, Sunrise.

Van Gogh knew how to be bolder,
using his dark blue willow tree trunks
to offset the wildfire of his Arles sunset.

If it were to be gone,
to disappear from the palette,
would we miss it? Do we need it?

Maybe not. But it's hard to imagine carrots, cantaloupes,
or peaches a different color. Tabby cats seem just right
being orange, as do monarch butterflies.

And let's not forget the blaze of autumn,
an annual reminder of glory
that reds and yellows cannot provide alone.

Giornata

A day's work.
Washing 45 windows of a skyscraper up near the clouds,
piloting 256 passengers on Alitalia from Rome to JFK,
performing one heart transplant,
preparing the dough for dozens of pizzas,
separating light from darkness,
writing six lines of a poem.

In Italian, the word for a day's work
comes from fresco mural painting.
The Old Masters could not dawdle.
Facing an empty section of wall
—an area about 4' by 5'—
they hurried every day, all day
to finish their *giornata*
while the plaster was still wet,
choosing this particular method
so the watercolors would soak in,
be absorbed into the wall,
be less vulnerable to scrapes or scratches
than if simply applied to a dry surface.

Much was at stake.
If Michelangelo, Raphael, or Giotto
did not complete the daily section,
the pigments in God's thumb
or on Gabriel's iridescent wing
might not match.

There are so many of us on the planet,
each one occupied with our own *giornata*,
filling our 4' by 5' squares day by day,
creating over a lifetime our unique versions
of the Sistine Chapel.

Seduction

One thing that doesn't interest me is porcelain,
not that I have anything against it,
my sink is porcelain,
I've heard of Meissen and Dresden,
and I should have some rose teacups
from my grandmother in a box somewhere,
but basically I'm just glad to ignore it,
leave it to others to enjoy, study, collect.

The same goes for fencing,
that tedious shimmy of two moonwalkers
jabbing at each other's space suits,
and when it comes to travels, there are places,
even entire countries, like Poland,
that are not on my list,
there has to be a lure, a promise of romance,
to cause me to pack my bags.
Prague has it, Gdansk not so much.

It's similar with art,
so today in Seattle I check my museum map
and head straight for Warhol's *Double Elvis*
and Pollock's *Sea Change* from his Drip Period.
Nearing the Elvises, I see on my right
a Porcelain Room, pass it by,
but there's a gleam,
and on a whim I turn around,
step inside,

and am taken back to 1967,
when I followed my Michelin Guide
to the Royal Portals, paused,
then entered a Gothic cathedral for the first time,
an American girl at Chartres, unprepared,
not expecting to be struck by glory,

to be exalted by something known as stained glass—
soaring medieval kaleidoscopes set in stone,
celestial architectural jewelry,
eternal roses in bloom.

And today the Porcelain Room
magnificent floor to ceiling,
every bit of wall space taken,
objects arranged to dazzle,
displayed in grand profusion,
many unusual, each with a story.
I pick out a Russian Bread Peddler
with a beard and heavy boots,
not dainty, offering me a loaf.

I'll study the history,
join the International Porcelain Society,
order catalogues from Sotheby's,
and make a list for my next museum visit,

beginning with the rarest piece, *Herons*,
a pair of intricately designed white birds
that are actually mythical phoenixes.

How inconvenient
to be seduced
by porcelain.

Welcome

It's my fault, I tell my husband glumly,
I forgot about the Seattle traffic, impossible
to get upstream that time of day.
We're late for my first poetry festival's
gala opening event, with no time
to pick up our tickets
or even open our umbrellas
as we search for the right building.

Finally outside the banquet room,
two wet salmon, inelegant, we peer in
on a hundred or more punctual people
chatting animatedly with Poets,
every seat is taken, waiters are offering
petit-fours and tarte flambées.

Then Molly—the festival Director we've not yet met—
comes out to greet us, her welcome as broad
as the Columbia River, she's so glad we've arrived,
dinner over? no worries, she'll speak with the chef,
and before we can apologize, her helpers
haul in a card table and two folding chairs,
then produce like magicians from their sleeves
a white tablecloth, place settings,
and a vase with fresh cut flowers.
Our dinner is served, the sommelier
filling our glasses with a flourish.

It's all my fault, I said to myself,
as the wrong train from Paris pulled in to Toulouse
three hours late, it was already dark, I was 18, alone,
a bit frightened, and when we entered the station
there was a man standing on the quai,
M. Henri Illaire, Director of the Institut de Français
in which I was enrolled, holding a small bouquet,
waiting for me, greeting me so warmly
in my nonexistent French, escorting me
to my room, leaving me that evening
not just with a thermos of coffee,
two boiled eggs, and a sandwich
his wife had packed in case I was hungry,
but with a love of France that would never diminish.

Bien venue, wil-cuma,
it is good you have come,
that's what Molly and Monsieur Illaire were saying
to me, not because of who I was,
but because of what the welcome is
from the moment we're born—

a bidding from someone already there
to cross
into the unknown
toward the new
an opening
an entrée
a defining thing.

Acknowledgments

The person who has accompanied me the entire way on this unpaved but scenic poetic journey is my husband Phillip Pirages. He has read and heard every poem in the book, responding to each new iteration with a wise heart and pen. One of the finest writers I know, Phil uses words beautifully, possessing an ability to make even minutes taken at a meeting entertaining. My poems are always the better for his inventive phrasing, off-beat humor, and infallible fine-tuning. For a decade now, he has done much to make poetry a joyful part of my daily life.

The second person I have been most fortunate to collaborate with is my professional editor, Matthew Lippman. By means of his thoughtful, sensitive, inspired assistance—poem by poem, page by page—this book has taken shape. Matthew is the rare editor whose critiques always feel uplifting, partly because he gives as much attention to letting you know what works—expressing his own excitement and enthusiasm freely—as he does to pointing out what probably doesn't. A gifted, often zany, and always bold poet, as well as a brilliant teacher, he has helped me take risks, improve my writing, and love even more the process of revision.

I also extend my thanks to the accomplished poet Abby Caplin for pointing me in Matthew's direction.

Finally, I am grateful to Andrea La Rue and Natalie Kimmel of Nectar Graphics for a cover design that, as their motto says, *tames the wild idea* so beautifully for me.

A note: The present book contains substantially revised poems from my three previous volumes, *Knotted* (2010), *In the same pod* (2013), and *Play on, words* (2015), as well as a selection of new poems.

As in the past, my proceeds from the sale of this book will go to the Give a Little Foundation (www.givealittlefoundation.org).

Made in the USA
San Bernardino, CA
13 September 2018